W9-CBQ-056

GREAT MINDS OF SCIENCE

BENJAMIN BANNEKER

Brilliant Surveyor, Mathematician, and Astronomer

by Erika Wittekind

Content Consultant
Sandra Perot
Lecturer, History
University of Massachusetts Amherst

Core Library

An Imprint of Abdo Publishing
abdopublishing.com

abdopublishing.com

Published by Abdo Publishing, a division of ABDO, PO Box 398166,
Minneapolis, Minnesota 55439. Copyright © 2016 by Abdo Consulting
Group, Inc. International copyrights reserved in all countries. No part of
this book may be reproduced in any form without written permission from
the publisher. Core Library™ is a trademark and logo of Abdo Publishing.

Printed in the United States of America, North Mankato, Minnesota
032015
092015

Cover Photo: Stock Montage/Getty Images
Interior Photos: Stock Montage/Getty Images, 1; North Wind Picture
Archives, 4, 6, 17, 20, 22, 34; Jim Plumb/iStockphoto, 8, 45; Shutterstock
Images, 12; iStockphoto, 14; Yuriy Kulik/Shutterstock Images, 19; NASA,
25; H. Bond and M. Barstow/ESA/NASA, 27; Carol M. Highsmith/Library of
Congress, 30, 43; Rembrandt Peale, 37; Public Domain, 38

Editor: Jenna Gleisner
Series Designer: Becky Daum

Library of Congress Control Number: 2015931126

Cataloging-in-Publication Data
Wittekind, Erika.
 Benjamin Banneker: Brilliant surveyor, mathematician, and astronomer /
Erika Wittekind.
    p. cm. -- (Great minds of science)
Includes bibliographical references and index.
ISBN 978-1-62403-870-9
1. Banneker, Benjamin, 1731-1806--Juvenile literature. 2. Astronomers-
-United States--Biography--Juvenile literature. 3. African American
scientists--Biography--Juvenile literature.   I. Title.
520.92--dc23
[B]   2015931126

CONTENTS

CHAPTER ONE

CURIOUS AT A YOUNG AGE

Living in Maryland in the early 1700s, Robert and Mary Banneky were not typical former slaves. They were among approximately 200 free African Americans living in Baltimore County at the time. The county's other 4,000 African Americans lived in slavery. Slaves worked for their owners for no pay. They had no freedom and often lived in poor conditions. But the Bannekys had their own tobacco

Benjamin Banneker grew up to become the country's first noted African-American scientist and mathematician.

Slaves, who were often forced to work on plantations, received no pay for their labor.

farm. On November 9, 1731, they welcomed their first child, a son they named Benjamin. Benjamin would grow up to become a prominent mathematician and astronomer. Later in life, he would use his position as a great thinker to challenge racism and slavery.

Banneka's Background

The Banneky family took its name from Benjamin's maternal grandfather, Banneka. The son of an African chief, Banneka had been captured in Africa and sold into slavery. After arriving in North America, Banneka was purchased by a white woman named Molly Welsh. Welsh had also arrived in the colonies against her will. Years before, Welsh had worked as a dairymaid in England. After knocking over a bucket of milk, she was transported, or sent, to the American colonies as an indentured servant. This meant she would

The Dogons

Some scholars believe Benjamin's grandfather, Banneka, may have belonged to a group called the Dogons before he was enslaved. The Dogons lived in western Africa in what is now Mali. They used advanced farming techniques, such as irrigation. They studied astronomy and were known for their accurate star charts. Banneka used this knowledge when he was living in America and passed it down to his family. Banneka's knowledge may have laid the foundation for some of Benjamin's scientific interests and ideas.

The Banneker family tended their own tobacco farm.

work for no pay for seven years before receiving her own land. In 1683 she arrived in the English colony of Maryland, where she went to work for a farmer.

At the end of her seven-year indenture, Welsh started her own tobacco farm. She bought two slaves to do farm work. One was Banneka. After several years, Welsh's farm was doing well and she was able to free her slaves. Soon after, Banneka and Welsh's relationship changed, and they started a family. Their daughter, Mary, grew up to marry a freed slave named Robert. Robert had no last name, so the couple used Mary's last name. They spelled it Banneky. The Bannekys lived on the family property until purchasing their own farm several years after Benjamin's birth.

A Young Mathematician

While Mary and Robert worked on the farm, Benjamin's grandmother Molly took care of him. He called her "Big Ma-Ma." She taught him to read and write using the only book she had, the Bible. She also taught him basic math. Benjamin learned quickly. He started figuring out more complicated math for himself. By the time he was six years old, family members and neighbors were asking him for help with

Patrollers

Even free African Americans lived in fear of being enslaved. White bounty hunters, called patrollers, looked for runaways. But they often targeted any African Americans they came across. If suspected runaways could not prove their freedom on the spot, they could be taken into custody. Then the patroller would sell them into slavery. When he was about eight years old, Benjamin and several other free African-American children were caught by a group of patrollers. Benjamin's grandmother lied to save them. She told the patrollers they were the children of her slave. Because she was white, the patrollers believed her. The children were all let go.

their accounting numbers. Benjamin corrected their errors. He could also recite all the figures from memory.

For one or two years of his childhood, Benjamin attended school with a small group of white and African-American children. His teacher, Peter Heinrich, recognized Benjamin's thirst for knowledge. Heinrich began loaning Benjamin books. Benjamin read as much as he could. He read books about history, science, and philosophy. He enjoyed reading more than playing with friends. Heinrich was so impressed that he suggested Benjamin use the last name Banneker. The teacher thought the name sounded more educated and would help Benjamin be taken seriously later in life.

Big Thoughts for a Young Boy

By the time Benjamin was 12, his father's health was failing. The family needed Benjamin to put down his books and help more on the farm. Benjamin spent long days working. He continued learning by observing the world around him. He recorded his observations in a diary. He thought about where the farm's soil came from. He noticed how the soil seemed to change as the crops sapped its nutrients year after year. He even wondered whether the soil on Earth was similar to soil on other planets. At the time, only the most educated people knew that Earth was part of a solar system that included other planets. It was a remarkable thought for a boy with little

Banneker speculated about other planets in our solar system.

schooling. But Benjamin Banneker would have many groundbreaking ideas during his lifetime.

Throughout his life, Benjamin Banneker continued to make observations of the natural world around him. He often noted these observations in his journals. In January 1797, Banneker wrote about some activity he saw in the beehives he was keeping on his farm:

> *On a pleasant day of the season, I observed my honeybees to be out of their hives, and they seemed very busy, all but one hive. Upon examination I found that all the bees had evacuated this hive, and left not a drop of honey behind them. On the 9th February ensuing, I killed the neighboring hives of bees, on a special occasion, and found a great quantity of honey, considering the season—which I imagine the stronger had violently taken from the weaker, and the weaker had pursued them to their home, resolved to be benefitted by their labour or die in the contest.*

Source: John H. B. Latrobe. "Memoir of Benjamin Banneker." Internet Archives. Internet Archives, 2014. Web. Accessed January 28, 2015.

What's the Big Idea?

Take a closer look at this passage. What did Banneker notice about the bees' behavior? What did he conclude based on his observations? What does his practice of writing down his observations tell you about Banneker's approach to science?

CHAPTER TWO

BANNEKER'S CLOCK

Banneker farmed on his family's land his whole life. In approximately 1753, when he was in his early 20s, he went to Baltimore to sell his family's tobacco crop. According to some accounts, Banneker met a man named Joseph Levi on this trip. The two men talked for hours about astronomy, gravity, and other scientific subjects. At the end of their talk, it is said that Levi took out a

Time-telling in the mid-1700s usually consisted of watching the shadows on a sundial.

African-American Farmers

Even though they were free and owned their own farm, Banneker's family struggled with racism. When Banneker was 22, he took a large harvest of quality tobacco leaves to sell in Baltimore. At the harbor, an official asked Banneker whether he had stolen the tobacco he was trying to sell. When Banneker said he had grown it, the man offered a much lower price than it was worth. Banneker tried to leave. But the official threatened to take it. Banneker was forced to sell for the lower price. Historians do not know if the details of this particular story are true. But it is typical of what an African-American farmer would have feared or experienced at the time.

pocket watch to check the time.

Most people did not have watches or clocks in the mid-1700s. They only knew approximate times of day by the sound of church bells or the position of the sun. Banneker had a sundial outside his cabin on the farm. As the sun moved across the sky, the shadow of a pointer moved across its face to give a rough idea of time. Levi's watch was the first real clock Banneker had seen. He was fascinated by it. He asked questions about

Transporting tobacco in the 1700s was difficult work.

how the watch's wheels moved to track minutes and seconds. Levi was impressed with Banneker's knowledge of mathematical concepts. He decided to let Banneker keep the watch.

Studying Time

Banneker studied the watch each day. At first he didn't open it because he didn't want to break it. But his curiosity grew every day. Finally he risked breaking

Timing the Cicada Cycle

Banneker realized that many things happen with regular increments of time. In 1749, when he was 17, Banneker noted that thousands of cicadas appeared on his farm's crops. The huge flock of insects appeared again 17 years later. During the decades he farmed, the locusts arrived on the same schedule. Banneker was among the earliest scientists to record the cicadas' 17-year life cycle.

the watch to see how it worked inside. He opened it to find it filled with tiny parts and gears. Right away Banneker could tell it had been made with special tools he didn't have. He realized he wouldn't be able to make one like it using simple farming tools. But he still wanted to understand more about the nature of time. He wanted to know how it could be measured and tracked by the ticking of this instrument. He decided to build a bigger version. He would have to make it out of wood, the one material he had access to.

Banneker observed and calculated the cycle of cicadas to determine when they would return to his family's crops.

From studying the little pocket watch, Banneker drew how its gears and parts connected. He used math to calculate the ratios, or relative sizes, of the gears to each other. As he made bigger parts, he had to keep the ratios the same. That way the larger clock would still track seconds, minutes, and hours correctly.

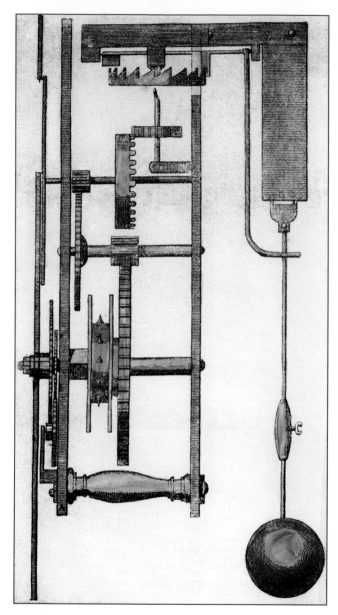

A Look Inside a 1700s Clock

Look closely at this diagram of a pendulum clock made in the early 1700s. Notice all of the gears. Imagine how they fit together to make a clock work. How does seeing this diagram help you better visualize the hard work Banneker performed to successfully build his own clock?

The project took Banneker several months. When he was done, he had succeeded in building the first clock made entirely of parts manufactured in America. Banneker's clock brought him into the spotlight. Word of it spread, and people started traveling to see it.

EXPLORE ONLINE

Chapter Two contains information about how people kept time in the 1700s. The website below gives more information about timekeeping in the 1700s. As you know, every source is different. How is the coverage of the subject on this website different from this chapter? What new information do you learn from this website? How does it affect your view of Banneker's interest in time and his building of a clock?

Keeping Nature's Time

mycorelibrary.com/benjamin-banneker

SEPTEMBER. IX Month.

In vain it is to plant, in vain to fow,
   In vain to harrow well the levell'd Plain,
If thou doft not command the Seed to grow,
   And give Increafe unto my bury'd Grain.
For not a fingle Corn will rufh to Birth,
Of all that I 've intrufted to the Earth,
If thou doft not enjoin the Shoot to fpring,
And the young Blade to full Perfection bring

		Remark. days, &c.	☉ rifɟ	☉ fet	☽ pl		Afpects, &c.
1	3	Dog-days end, ♃	5 32	6 28	♐	11	♀ fets 8 1
2	4	*Windy and*	5 33	6 27		24	*Good Men*
3	5	Day break 4 12	5 34	6 26	♑	7	*from Vice,*
4	6	*fair, then*	5 35	6 25		21	7*s rife 9 13
5	7	*warm, with*	5 36	6 24	♒	6	♄ rifes 11 57
6	D	12 paft Trin.	5 38	6 22		21	☌ ☉ ♂ *for*
7	2	*clouds, and*	5 39	6 21	♓	6	✶ ♀ ☿ *Love*
8	3	Nativ. *V. M.*	5 40	6 20		21	Sirius rife 2 22
9	4	*like for rain:*	5 41	6 19	♈	6	*of Virtue, run,*
10	5	Day dec. 2 16	5 43	6 17		21	*But Fear*
11	6	*foggy mornings,*	5 44	6 16	♉	6	*alone makes*
12	7	*then clear,*	5 46	6 14		20	♃ fets 6 43
13	D	13 paft Trin.	5 47	6 13	♊	4	7*s rife 8 40
14	2	Holy Rood.	5 49	6 11		17	✶ ♄ ☿
15	3	Swan's Tail.	5 50	6 10	♋	0	☽ with ♄
16	4	Ember Week.	5 51	6 9		13	△ ♄ ♀
17	5	*with warm funs,*	5 53	6 7		25	♀ fets 7 21
18	6	*temperate,*	5 54	6 6	♌	7	Sirius rif
19	7	*clouds, with*					

CHAPTER THREE

STUDYING THE STARS

In 1758 Banneker's father died. Banneker was now in charge of the farm. He spent roughly the next decade dedicating himself to farm work. He had little time for science. Then in the early 1770s, he took an interest in a family that was building a mill to turn wheat into flour. Banneker began visiting the Ellicott mill. He wanted to study its machinery. This was how he met George Ellicott, who was studying astronomy.

Astronomy and weather patterns were charted in almanacs in the 1700s.

The two quickly became friends. Ellicott loaned Banneker astronomy books and gave him a telescope to use.

Ellicott's Mill

Ellicott's mill brought the Industrial Revolution to Banneker's neighborhood. The Industrial Revolution refers to the changes in manufacturing and farming technology that began in approximately 1760. The Ellicotts used new machinery in their mills that made the process of turning wheat into flour more efficient. Their mill brought other industries to the area as well. Companies were needed to make iron products, furnaces, wagon parts, and tools. The town that sprang up was called Ellicott's Mills, and later Ellicott City.

Ellicott and Banneker studied books written by two leading astronomers of the time, James Ferguson and Charles Leadbetter. These two astronomers disagreed about the positions of the sun and moon during a lunar eclipse. The moon can usually be seen because the sun lights parts of it. During a lunar eclipse, Earth's shadow blocks the sunlight. This means the moon appears fully or partially

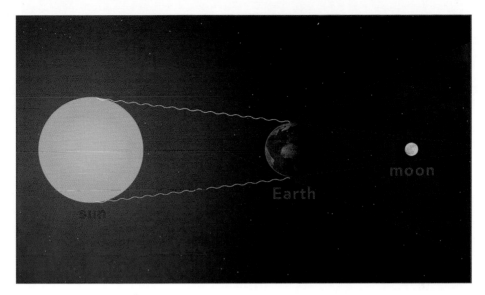

Total Lunar Eclipse

Look closely at this diagram of a total lunar eclipse. During an eclipse, the sun, Earth, and the moon line up in space. The sun shines on Earth, casting a shadow that covers the moon. When the moon moves directly into Earth's shadow, a total eclipse occurs. How does seeing this diagram better help you understand Banneker's studies of astronomy?

covered. Banneker figured out that both Ferguson and Leadbetter were wrong about the positions of the sun and moon. Banneker's more accurate figures were published in the *Atlantic Monthly* close to a century later, in 1863. He did not have the formal education or fine instruments of Ferguson or Leadbetter. But Banneker had come to the right conclusion.

Astronomical Discoveries

In the coming years, Banneker made more breakthroughs in astronomy. In several cases he was more than a century ahead of other scientists. Banneker guessed that every star in the sky was like Earth's sun. He thought that each star was probably circled by its own set of planets. His theory was based on the fact that patterns tend to be repeated throughout the natural world. This was long before modern methods confirmed in 1943 that planets exist around other stars.

Banneker was the first person to write that a bright star called Sirius is actually two stars, each with a different brightness. National Aeronautics and Space Administration (NASA) scientists confirmed this two centuries later using the Hubble Space Telescope. Banneker was also the first US scientist to write about the possibility of life on other planets. He figured that, with so many planets in the universe, some of them

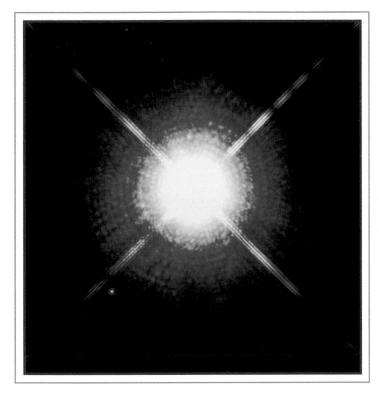

Banneker was the first person to document that Sirius was actually two stars.

must contain life. This idea was almost unheard of at the time.

Creating an Almanac

Banneker still farmed during the day. But at night, he stayed up late to watch the sky and record his observations and calculations. He often slept late. Because of this, some of his neighbors thought he'd grown lazy. But he was working harder than ever. With his eyes on the sky, Banneker decided he wanted to put his knowledge to more practical use. He began writing his own almanac. An almanac is a book that is published each year. Almanacs contain important dates, astronomical charts, and information on tides. Charts show where the moon and planets will appear in the sky on different dates. Sailors used these charts to figure out their location. Farmers used information from almanacs to predict weather patterns. These books also often included essays, humor, and sayings.

Writing an almanac required Banneker to be knowledgeable on many subjects. He performed many complicated calculations to make charts of the stars and

Feeding the Troops

In 1776 the American colonies declared independence from Britain, beginning the American Revolutionary War (1775–1783). Banneker had high hopes that independence from Britain would bring an end to slavery. He even tried to serve in the military but was turned down due to his age. Banneker was 45 at the time. He later converted his tobacco farm to a wheat farm after hearing that the military needed more food.

planets. It would be several years until Banneker achieved his goal of publishing his own almanac. By 1791 his almanac was almost ready. But before he could have it printed, an unexpected opportunity called Banneker away.

FURTHER EVIDENCE

This chapter covers Banneker's work in astronomy and how that led him to write an almanac. What is a main point of the chapter? What evidence in the chapter supports that point? Visit the website below to read more about Banneker's almanac. Find a quote in the article that supports this chapter's main point. Does it support an existing piece of evidence in the chapter? Or does it add a new one?

Benjamin Banneker's *Almanac*
mycorelibrary.com/benjamin-banneker

CHAPTER FOUR

NATIONAL RECOGNITION

After the Revolutionary War, the American colonies won their independence from Britain. George Washington became the new country's first president. He chose a location for the national capital in 1791. It would be on a small area of land between Virginia and Maryland, on the Potomac River. Washington chose Frenchman Pierre L'Enfant to design the city. L'Enfant selected Andrew

Banneker surveyed and mapped out the nation's capital using his knowledge of astronomy and mathematics.

Ellicott, the uncle of George Ellicott, to be the project's chief surveyor. Land surveyors observe and measure land, set up boundaries, and prepare maps. Andrew Ellicott selected a team to help him with the work. Surprising everyone, he hired an African-American man—his old friend Benjamin Banneker.

Mapping the Capital

Banneker had no experience in this sort of work other than reading about it in a book. But George Ellicott told his uncle that Banneker was the best man for the job. The reason was Banneker's expertise in astronomy. The surveyors needed known reference points to plot boundaries. But the area where the city would be built was wilderness at the time. The surveyors had few recognizable landmarks down on Earth. So they needed to figure out their exact positions by calculating the angles to known stars. It was complicated work.

Banneker had to take into account Earth's rotation. Measurements had to be taken at precise times. Changing temperatures could affect the accuracy of the time readings, so Banneker set up several thermometers. Using his knowledge of astronomy, the scientist kept the survey work on track.

A Call to Speak

Banneker completed his work on the capital in two months. He then returned home to Maryland. Banneker realized the work he was doing could serve another purpose. He knew that many African Americans were

Fact or Fiction?

A story has often been repeated about Banneker's role in designing Washington, DC. After Pierre L'Enfant left the project, he refused to turn over the original copy of his plan. According to the story, Banneker had seen the architect's plan once and committed it completely to memory. He recreated the entire plan from scratch. Historians now question this version. They think it is unlikely only one copy of the city plan existed. It is more likely that Ellicott's team pieced the plan back together from smaller sections and drafts.

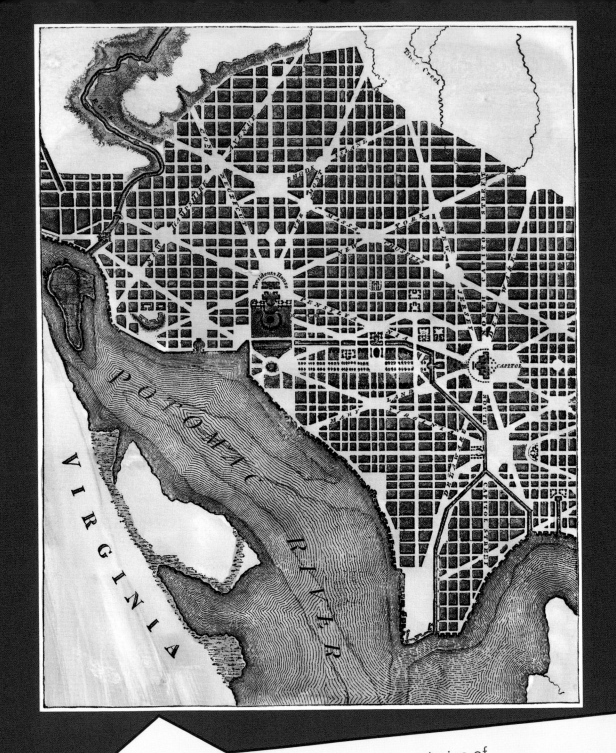

Banneker and his team mapped the boundaries of the capital, as well as the locations of key streets and buildings.

still enslaved. Even those who lived free faced unfair treatment due to their race. Many whites still believed that African Americans were inferior. Earlier in his life, Banneker had preferred to devote himself to science rather than speak out on these issues. But now he had played a key role in building the country's capital. And he was about to become the first African-American scientist to publish an almanac. He felt he was in a position to do more.

Banneker got to work updating the astronomical charts for his first almanac. It would be for the year 1792. He added essays and humorous stories. At first he had trouble finding a printer for the book. Many refused to print a book written by an African-American man. But abolitionists—people who wanted to end slavery—helped him find a printer. The abolitionists wanted the country to find out about Banneker's work.

Publishing the First Almanac

With this in mind, Banneker sent an advance copy of the almanac to Thomas Jefferson in August 1791. Jefferson, who was secretary of state, had approved Banneker to assist on the survey project earlier that year. He had also written that African Americans had less intelligence than whites. Along with his almanac, Banneker sent a letter to Jefferson. The letter argued against slavery and racism. He offered his own work as proof that skill had nothing to do with race. The letter quoted Jefferson's own words from the Declaration of Independence. Jefferson had written that "all men are created equal." Banneker asked Jefferson to extend that thought to all races. His letter and Jefferson's reply were both included in later printings of that first almanac. Now everyone could read the debate.

Banneker's 1792 almanac was a huge success. With the money he made from it, Banneker was able to cut down on his farm work. He could devote more time to studying the stars and working on the next

In his almanac, Banneker addressed Thomas Jefferson directly on the issue of race and equality.

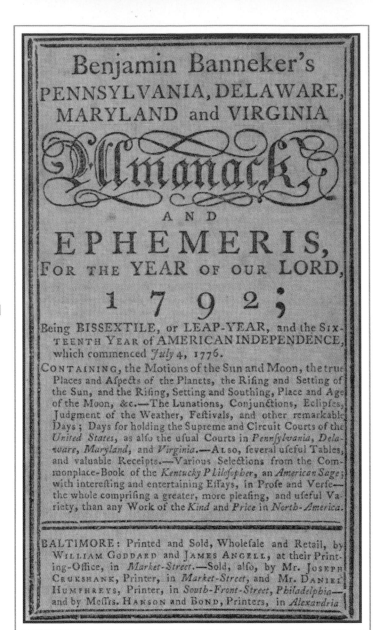

Banneker published his first almanac in 1792.

year's almanac. The almanac also earned Banneker

respect in the scientific community. He continued

publishing an almanac every year until 1797. Over the

years, he included more essays that argued for an end to slavery and for the equal treatment of African Americans.

Banneker stopped publishing the almanac after 1797. By that point, his health was declining. He continued making the astronomical charts for his own study and enjoyment. His books, letters from his readers, and many visitors also kept him busy. In 1806 Banneker fell ill and died at the age of 74. During his funeral, his cabin burned down. It is believed that his

Early Review

Before printing his first almanac, Banneker sent his charts to a well-respected astronomer, David Rittenhouse, to check his work. Rittenhouse approved Banneker's calculations. But his reply showed the disbelief felt by many at the time that an African-American man was capable of complicated scientific work. Rittenhouse wrote to Banneker, "I think the papers I herewith return to you a very extraordinary performance, considering the [color] of the Author." Banneker did not think his race had anything to do with his work. "The work is either correct or it is not," he responded.

enemies—people who disagreed with his views on slavery—set it on fire. Banneker's clocks and many of his papers burned. While much of his life's work was lost, he is recognized as a remarkable scientist. In addition to his many scientific achievements, he is considered one of the country's first civil rights leaders. He paved the way for scientists and mathematicians of all races who came after him.

In 1791 Banneker sent a copy of his almanac to Thomas Jefferson. In a long letter, Banneker argued that the races should be equal and that slavery should be ended. Jefferson responded, commenting on Banneker's abilities and knowledge:

Nobody wishes more than I do to see such proofs as you exhibit, that nature has given to our black brethren talents equal to those of the other [colors] of men, and that the appearance of a want of them is owing to the degraded condition of their existence both in Africa and America. I can add with truth that no one wishes more ardently to see a good system commenced for raising the condition both of their body and mind to what it ought to be, as fast as the imbecility of their present existence, and other circumstances which cannot be neglected, will admit.

Source: John H. B. Latrobe. "Memoir of Benjamin Banneker." Internet Archives. Internet Archives, 2014. Web. Accessed January 28, 2015.

Point of View

After reading Jefferson's response, compare it to what you read about Banneker's letter in this chapter. What is the point of view of each letter writer? How does each approach the topic of race? Write a short essay comparing the two points of view presented in the letters.

Mapping the Capital

With little formal education, Benjamin Banneker used his observational skills and logic to make discoveries long before other astronomers. Based on his knowledge of patterns, for example, he guessed that every star in the sky was like Earth's sun, with its own set of planets in orbit. This was not proved until almost two centuries later. Banneker's knowledge in astronomy also helped play a key role in designing the capital city of Washington, DC. As a member of the surveying team, he used his knowledge of the stars to help identify locations for boundaries and future roads and buildings.

Creating the Almanac

Benjamin Banneker published a series of popular almanacs from 1792 to 1797. These almanacs contained important dates, astronomical charts, and information on tides. The charts show where the moon and planets will appear in the sky on different dates throughout the year. Almanacs are still produced and used today. For example, farmers refer to information from almanacs to predict weather patterns.

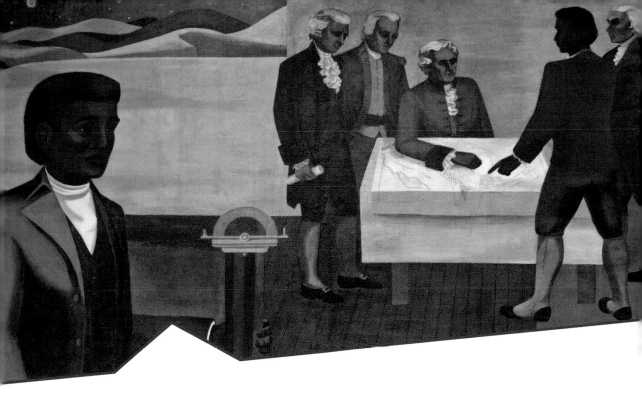

Fighting for Equality

Benjamin Banneker's almanacs helped prove to white skeptics that race was not a factor in scientific ability. Along with his first almanac, he included his correspondence with Thomas Jefferson on slavery as well as other essays on the subject. As the first African-American scientist to gain respect and recognition, Banneker paved the way for future scientists of all races. He is also considered one of the country's first civil rights leaders.

Say What?

Learning about science can mean learning a lot of new vocabulary. Find five words in this book that you have never seen or heard before. Use a dictionary to look up their meanings. Write out the definitions in your own words, and then use each word in a sentence.

Take a Stand

Pretend you are an abolitionist living in the 1700s. You have just learned of Benjamin Banneker's scientific work. How could you use him as an example of why African Americans and whites should have equal rights? Write a short essay that supports your position.

Why Do I Care?

Benjamin Banneker lived more than 200 years ago. But that doesn't mean you can't find similarities between his work and your life. Why is his scientific work still important? Have any of his breakthroughs affected your own life?

You Are There

This book discusses the scientific contributions of Benjamin Banneker. If you were a friend of Banneker, what questions would you have about his work? What would you want him to teach you more about? How could you help him in his research?

GLOSSARY

almanac
a book published annually
that contains information
about the stars and planets,
tides, and other topics

astronomy
the scientific study of stars,
planets, and other objects in
outer space

boundaries
imaginary lines that show
where one area ends and
another area begins

civil rights
the rights a person should
have regardless of race,
gender, or religion

gravity
the natural force that causes
objects to fall toward Earth

lunar
relating to the moon

racism
poor treatment of people
because of their race, or the
belief that one race is inferior
to another

ratio
the relationship between the
size or number of two things

surveyor
a person whose job is to
measure and assess land

LEARN MORE

Books

Rissman, Rebecca. *Slavery in the United States.* Minneapolis: ABDO Publishing, 2015.

Rodgers, Kelly. *Our Nation's Capital: Washington, DC.* Huntington Beach, CA: Teacher Created Materials, 2015.

Websites

To learn more about Great Minds of Science, visit **booklinks.abdopublishing.com**. These links are routinely monitored and updated to provide the most current information available.

Visit **mycorelibrary.com** for free additional tools for teachers and students.

INDEX

ABOUT THE AUTHOR

Erika Wittekind is a freelance writer and editor who lives in Wisconsin. She has written nearly one dozen books for children on a variety of topics.